LET'S GET COOKING!

Fun with

ITALIAN Cooking

Rosalba Gioffrè

PowerKiDS press™

New York

Published in 2010 by The Rosen Publishing Group, Inc.
29 East 21st Street, New York, NY 10010

U.S. Editor: Kara Murray

Photo Credits: All images by Marco Lanza and Walter Mericchi.

Library of Congress Cataloging-in-Publication Data

Gioffrè, Rosalba.
  Fun with Italian cooking / Rosalba Gioffrè.
      p. cm. — (Let's get cooking!)
  Includes index.
  ISBN 978-1-4358-3451-4 (library binding) — ISBN 978-1-4358-3489-7 (pbk.) — ISBN 978-1-4358-3490-3 (6-pack)
  1. Cookery, Italian—Juvenile literature. 2. Food habits—Italy—Juvenile literature. I. Title.
  TX723.G4777 2010
  641.5945—dc22

                          2009010339

Printed in China

Contents

Introduction

Italian food is not only delicious, it is also easy to prepare. This makes it especially good for young chefs. In this book, there are 14 popular recipes with step-by-step photographs. By following the instructions carefully, you can surprise your friends and family with some delicious food. Each recipe also has special tips and tricks to help a young chef get it right. Pages 18–19 tell you about *Carnevale*, showing the fun and the food that Italian children enjoy at that time of year. So, have fun, or as they say in Italy, *Buon divertimento*!

When cooking, you should always have an adult with you in the kitchen to help. Many of the tools used to prepare these recipes and others can be dangerous. Always be very careful when using a knife or a stove.

Bruschetta
(broos-KET-ah)

This delicious summer snack is served all over Italy, but it is especially popular in the south, where tomatoes are plentiful. This dish can be made with other vegetables, such as red peppers, but here we use only tomatoes.

Ingredients

2 thick slices of crusty white bread

2 cloves garlic, peeled

6 fresh basil leaves

2 tablespoons extra-virgin olive oil

salt and ground black pepper to taste

2 large ripe salad tomatoes

Rinse your fingertips in a little vinegar to remove the strong smell of garlic.

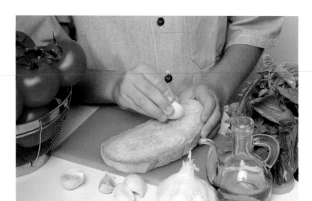

1 Toast two slices of bread until they are a light golden brown. Rub each slice with a clove of garlic. The crispy surface of the bread will quickly absorb the garlic.

Utensils

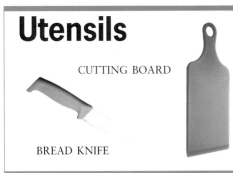

CUTTING BOARD

BREAD KNIFE

2 Rinse the tomatoes and wipe them dry with paper towels. Chop the tomatoes into cubes and spread them over the bread. Be very careful with the knife. You do not need a very sharp one. An ordinary bread knife is fine.

3 Rinse the basil and shake lightly until dry. Use your fingertips to tear the basil into pieces and **sprinkle** it over the tomatoes. Season with a little salt.

TIPS & TRICKS

Bruschetta makes a healthy after-school snack. The recipe given here will be enough for one or two. Spread the mixture on the bread just before serving so that the bread does not become soggy. Ask an adult to help when working with knives.

4 **Drizzle** the bruschetta with olive oil to taste. For a little extra flavor, sprinkle black pepper over the top.

Crostini

(kruh-STEE-nee)

You may be unfamiliar with some of the ingredients in this recipe, but don't worry, the chicken livers and **anchovies** combine with the other ingredients to make a delicious topping. This dish is found all over Italy, but originally comes from Tuscany, where it is served as an antipasto, or **appetizer**, along with a plate of ham and salami.

Ingredients

10 ounces (300 g) chicken livers, cleaned and fat removed

2 anchovies (from a can, preserved in oil)

2 tablespoons capers

salt (just a little—the anchovies and capers are already salty)

1 small red onion, **coarsely chopped**

4 tablespoons extra-virgin olive oil

1 baguette, or French bread

TIPS & TRICKS

You will need a sharp knife to chop the chicken livers and onion. Be very careful while doing this. Hold the knife up on the handle and keep your fingers away from the blade. Ask an adult to help. Many cooks in Italy use a half-moon chopper because it is much safer for chopping.

1 Use a bread knife with a **serrated** blade to slice the bread into pieces about ½ in (1 cm) thick. Toast lightly.

HALF-MOON
CHOPPER

CUTTING
BOARD

FOOD MILL
OR FOOD
PROCESSOR

FRYING
PAN

2 Rinse the chicken livers and chop coarsely. Cook in a frying pan over high heat for 1 minute. Then add the oil, onion, anchovies, and capers. Cook for 3 to 4 minutes. Pour in ½ cup (125 ml) hot water, and cook for 8 to 10 more minutes.

3 Add salt if necessary. Remove the frying pan from the heat and put the mixture into a food processor or food mill with 2 tablespoons of warm water. Blend until creamy.

4 Spread the mixture on the toasted bread. Arrange the toast on a dish and serve.

Margherita Pizza

(mahr-guh-REE-tuh)

Making pizza is simple and fun. The two most important things to remember when making pizza are to **knead** the dough properly and leave it long enough to rise. This recipe is for a Margherita pizza, which was invented in 1889 for Queen Margherita of Savoy, a region that includes parts of what is now France and Italy. You can also add ham, mushrooms, or any topping you like.

1 In a small bowl, **dissolve** the yeast in 2 tablespoons of warm water, mixing well. Put the yeast aside for 15 minutes. Put the flour and salt into a large bowl.

2 Gradually work the yeast mixture into the flour. Flour your hands and use your knuckles and fists to work the dough until it is smooth and stretchy.

3 Form the dough into a ball, and wrap it loosely in a clean cotton cloth. Leave it in the bowl in a warm, sheltered place to rise for at least 30 minutes. Preheat the oven to 450 °F (230 °C).

4 Oil a rectangular or circular pizza tray and use your fingertips to gently stretch the dough out to cover the bottom.

5 Open the can of tomatoes, pour them into a bowl and chop them. Spread them evenly over the dough. Cut the mozzarella into small pieces and sprinkle it over the tomatoes.

6 Sprinkle with the oregano. Drizzle with the oil and bake in the oven for about 20 minutes.

Ingredients

3 cups (400 g) all-purpose flour

½ teaspoon salt

cherry-sized lump baker's yeast or **1½ level tablespoons** dried yeast

14-ounce (400 g) can of plum tomatoes

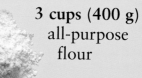

5 ounces (150 g) mozzarella

2 tablespoons extra-virgin olive oil

pinch of fresh or dried oregano

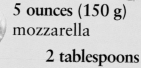

Utensils

MIXING BOWL

PIZZA TRAY

TIPS & TRICKS

Ask an adult to open the can of tomatoes and also to take the pizza out of the oven. If you do handle the hot pizza tray yourself, make sure you wear thick oven mitts to protect your hands.

Penne with Tomato Sauce

Pasta is the national dish in Italy, where it is served every day. Tomato sauce is one of the most popular toppings for pasta. Tomatoes were brought to Italy from Mexico and Central America by Spanish explorers during the 16th century. When you serve the dish, say *Buon appetito!*, which means "Enjoy!"

Ingredients

14-ounce (400 g) can of tomatoes

or

1 pound (500 g) fresh tomatoes

6 fresh basil leaves, torn into pieces

2 cloves garlic, peeled and chopped

1 pound (500 g) penne

4 tablespoons extra-virgin olive oil

2 ounces (60 g) grated Parmesan

pinch of salt for the sauce

If you have some sauce left over, spoon it over a slice of toasted bread for a tasty snack.

1 Bring a large saucepan of water to boil. Drain the canned tomatoes, put them in a separate saucepan and mash them with a fork. If fresh tomatoes are used, ask an adult to help you skin and chop them and place them in the pan.

Utensils

SPOON

SAUCEPANS

COLANDER

SERVING DISH

CHEESE GRATER

2 Add the olive oil, garlic, and salt to the tomatoes. Place the pan over medium heat and cook for about 20 minutes, stirring often to prevent sticking. Remove from the heat and add the basil.

3 When the water in the pan is boiling, add the pasta. Cook for the amount of time shown on the package, stirring occasionally. Drain the pasta in the colander and place on the serving dish.

4 Spoon the tomato sauce over the cooked pasta and mix well. Sprinkle the grated Parmesan over the pasta. Serve immediately.

This sauce is good with all pasta shapes, including spaghetti, macaroni, and rigatoni. You can try it with whole wheat or spinach pasta, too.

TIPS & TRICKS

Be very careful when draining the pasta. The large pan of boiling water and pasta will be very heavy. Ask an adult to help you lift it. The trick with pasta is getting the cooking time right. It should be soft but still firm when you chew it. Do not cook it so much that it gets mushy and tasteless!

Tagliatelle with Ham

(tahl-yah-TEL-ay)

Tagliatelle is a type of pasta that comes from an area called Emilia-Romagna in central Italy. It should be ⅓ inch (8 mm) wide. If it is wider than this, it is known as *pappadelle*, and if it is thinner, it is called *tagliolini*. The sauce is also a recipe from Emilia-Romagna. It features delicious Parma ham, called prosciutto, which is a specialty of the city of Parma in Emilia-Romagna.

1 Bring a large saucepan of water to boil. Put the prosciutto on a cutting board. Cut it first into strips and then into squares. Hold the knife firmly in one hand and keep your fingers away from the blade.

Ingredients

1 pound (500 g) fresh or dried tagliatelle

5 ounces (150 g) prosciutto

1 pound (500 g) fresh or canned tomatoes

8 tablespoons (125 g) butter

pinch of salt

3 ounces (90 g) Parmesan

TIPS & TRICKS

Always turn the handle of pots and pans on the stove in so that you do not knock them over. Place the large pan of boiling water for the pasta on a burner on the back of the stove, where it is safer.

2 Ask an adult to help you skin the tomatoes, then chop them roughly, or open a can of tomatoes and mash them in a bowl using a fork. Place the tomatoes in another saucepan, together with the prosciutto and the butter.

3 Mix well and cook over medium heat for about 30 minutes. Stir occasionally with a wooden spoon. Add salt to taste.

4 While the sauce is cooking, add the tagliatelle to the boiling water. Follow the instructions on the package for the correct cooking time. Grate the Parmesan.

5 When the pasta is cooked, drain it in a colander. Place in a large serving dish. Ladle the sauce over the top and sprinkle with the Parmesan. Toss well and serve.

Utensils

LADLE

CHEESE GRATER

KNIFE

CUTTING BOARD

TWO LARGE SAUCEPANS

WOODEN SPOON

Pasta with Pesto

This pasta sauce is quick and easy to make. You just have to mix the ingredients in a food processor, cook the pasta, combine the two and serve! Pesto comes from Genoa, on the Italian Riviera, an area on the Mediterranean coast. Genoa has a mild climate where herbs, such as basil, grow especially well.

Utensils

MIXING SPOONS

HANDHELD FOOD PROCESSOR

CHEESE GRATER

COLANDER

1 Bring a large saucepan of water to boil. Separate the basil leaves from the stems. Place the leaves in a colander and rinse them. Drain well and dry on a clean cloth.

2 Grate the cheeses. If you have one, use a grater with a little dish underneath so that it is easier to collect the grated cheese.

Ingredients

1 ounce (30 g) toasted pine nuts

40 fresh basil leaves

12 ounces (340 g) linguine

pinch of salt

1 cup (150 ml) extra-virgin olive oil

1 clove garlic

1 ounce (30 g) of both Parmesan and pecorino

3 Place the basil, cheeses, pine nuts, garlic, oil, and salt in a bowl and chop with a handheld food processor. If you use a large food processor, place the ingredients in it and mix everything around until the sauce is creamy.

4 When the water in the saucepan is boiling, add the pasta. Cook for the amount of time shown on the package. Take 2 tablespoons of the water from the pan and place it in a serving dish. Drain the pasta in the colander and place in the serving dish. Pour the pesto over the pasta and toss well. Serve immediately.

TIPS & TRICKS

When using a food processor, make sure your hands are completely dry. Never put your fingers inside the processor or near the blade of a handheld processor. To scrape the mixture off the sides of the processor, turn it off and use a spatula. Ask an adult to help you.

Gnocchi with Meat Sauce

(NYOH-kee)

These little potato dumplings are people all over Italy's favorite dish. They can be served with a variety of sauces or even in soup. Gnocchi originally came from Verona, in northern Italy, where they were served with melted butter, sugar, and cinnamon. In Tuscany, they are called *topini*, which means "little mice."

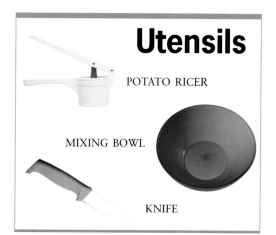

Utensils

POTATO RICER

MIXING BOWL

KNIFE

1 Cook the unpeeled potatoes in a large pan of boiling water. Drain and set aside. When cool, remove the skins using your fingers, then mash.

2 Dust your hands with flour and begin working the flour and salt into the mashed potatoes. Continue until the mixture is smooth and well mixed but still soft.

Ingredients

2 pounds (1 kg) potatoes

2 cups (250 g) all-purpose flour

pinch of salt

14 ounce- (400 g) jar of Italian meat sauce

2 ounces (60 g) grated Parmesan

3 Take a handful of the mixture and roll it out into a long, thin sausage on a floured work surface. Cut the sausage into lengths about 1 inch (2.5 cm) long. Bring a big saucepan of water to boil.

4 Pick up each gnocchi in one hand and run the tines of a fork along the edges so that it has lines running around it. If this is too hard or takes too long, leave this step out. The gnocchi will still taste great anyway.

5 Place the gnocchi on a lightly floured cloth. When the water is boiling, add the first batch of gnocchi. When they float to the top, they are cooked. Scoop them out with a slotted spoon, and put them on a serving dish. Repeat until all the gnocchi are cooked. Heat the meat sauce and pour over the gnocchi. Sprinkle with the Parmesan and serve.

TIPS & TRICKS

To avoid being splashed by boiling water, place the gnocchi on a small, lightly floured dish, dip the edge into the water, and let them slip gently into the pan.

Carnevale

(kahr-nay-VAHL-ay)

Carnevale, "carnival" in English, is a holiday celebrated in many **Roman Catholic** countries before Lent. In Italy, the most important celebrations are held in the week leading up to Shrove Tuesday. After that comes Ash Wednesday and the start of the 40 days of Lent. To host an Italian Carnevale party, prepare the *cenci* (this is the Tuscan name for these sweets; they are prepared all over Italy, but have different names). Have your friends dress up. Make papier-mâché masks and paint them in bright colors. Many people also throw **confetti** and even spray people with shaving cream! The best day to have your Carnevale party is Shrove Tuesday.

This mask is one of many worn at carnival time in Venice.

Cenci

- **2 cups (250 g)** all-purpose flour
- **2 tablespoons (30 g)** softened butter
- **2 eggs**
- **¼ cup (60 g)** sugar
- **pinch** of salt
- **2 tablespoons** grated orange zest
- **1 cup (250 ml)** olive oil for frying
- **1/4 cup (60 g)** confectioners' sugar

Sift the flour into a bowl and add the butter, eggs, sugar, salt, and orange zest. Stir with a wooden spoon, then knead with your hands until the dough is smooth and stretchy. Cover with a clean cloth and leave for 30 minutes. Roll out into a thin sheet and cut into rectangular strips, some of which can be tied into loose knots. Heat the oil in a deep frying pan and fry the cenci a few at a time until they are golden brown. Ask an adult to help you. Remove them with a slotted spoon and drain on paper towels. Sprinkle with the confectioners' sugar and serve at once.

There are many costumes you can wear at carnival time. In the past, people wore masks so they could poke fun at their rulers without fear of being recognized or punished for it.

These people are celebrating Carnevale in Piazza San Marco in the northern Italian city of Venice. Carnevale in Venice has become so famous that people from all over the world visit at this time.

Boys often used to wear brightly colored Harlequin costumes, such as this one. Harlequin, Arlecchino in Italian, was a well-known character in Italian theater in the sixteenth and seventeenth centuries. Girls often dressed up as fairies. Today, both boys and girls wear costumes based on their favorite movies or TV shows.

Risotto
(ree-SOHT-toh)

Rice was introduced to Western Europe by **Arabs** during the **Middle Ages**. Risotto was invented in the northern Italian city of Milan, where it is still eaten often. To prepare risotto, you cook the rice slowly, so that it absorbs the flavors of all the other ingredients. **Saffron** adds a touch of color, turning the rice red or gold, depending on how much you add.

Ingredients

1 medium red onion

4 tablespoons (60 g) butter

14 ounces (400 g) rice (preferably Italian Arborio rice)

3½ cups (1 l) chicken stock, made with boiling water and 1 bouillon cube

1 packet saffron

3 ounces (90 g) grated Parmesan

1 Chop the onion coarsely using a half-moon chopper or knife. In a large saucepan, **sauté** the onion in half the butter until it is golden.

2 Add the rice to the saucepan and stir constantly over medium heat for about 2 minutes. Hold the saucepan firmly by the handle while stirring. The rice should swell and be lightly toasted.

Utensils

HALF-MOON CHOPPER

LADLE

CHEESE GRATER

CUTTING BOARD

WOODEN SPOON

LARGE SAUCEPAN

3 Dissolve the bouillon cube in the hot water. Begin adding the stock to the rice a ladleful at a time, stirring as it is absorbed by the rice.

4 Continue cooking and gradually adding more stock for about 20 minutes. Stir all the time so that the rice does not stick to the pan. Taste the rice after about 15 minutes to see if it is cooked. It should be soft but firm, or *al dente,* which means "firm to the bite."

5 When the rice is cooked, remove from the heat and stir in the remaining butter.

6 Add the saffron and mix well so that the rice is evenly colored. Finally, stir in the Parmesan and serve.

Meatballs

These meatballs will become one of your favorite dishes. The bread swells during cooking, making them soft as well as tasty. You can eat them with a fork. These are also fun to make because you can do it all with your hands. You squeeze the soft ground meat together with the other ingredients and then form it into balls.

2 Grate the cheese and bread together into a large bowl. Keep your fingertips away from the grater.

1 Combine the tomato puree, salt, and oil in a large saucepan. Cook over low heat for about 15 minutes, stirring often.

Utensils

GRATER

DEEP FRYING PAN

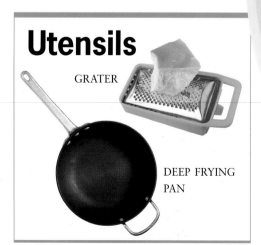

3 Combine the meat with the bread, cheese, eggs, salt, and pepper in a large mixing bowl. Mix well with your hands. Add a ladleful of the tomato sauce and stir it in with a spoon. Let the mixture cool.

4 Rinse your hands in cold water to keep the mixture from sticking to them. Use your hands to form the mixture into smooth round balls about the size of large plums. Repeat this step until there is no more mixture left. Place the meatballs on a plate.

5 Add the meatballs carefully to the tomato sauce, one at a time. Cook them in the sauce over low heat for 20 to 30 minutes without stirring. Shake the pan very gently from time to time. Serve the meatballs with pasta or rice.

Ingredients

5 cups (1.5 l) tomato puree

pinch of salt

¼ cup (60 ml) extra-virgin olive oil

1 pound (500 g) ground beef

1 loaf Italian bread

3 eggs

8 ounces (250 g) grated Parmesan

pinch of black pepper

TIPS & TRICKS

Add the meatballs to the sauce very gently so that they don't break or splash sauce on you. A good way to do this is to dip a tablespoon into cold water and use it to pick up each meatball and then slip it into the pan.

Fish Dish!

This dish tastes good even if you don't usually like fish. The strong flavor of the fish is softened a little by the potatoes and mayonnaise. It is also fun to make because you can mold the fish mixture with your hands to create the shape of a fish. Garnish your fish with mayonnaise, adding a mouth, gills, scales, and tail.

Utensils

COLANDER

POTATO RICER

BOWL

1 Boil the potatoes in a pan of salted water for about 25 minutes or until tender. Drain in a colander. When they have cooled a little, use your fingers to peel off the skins.

2 Put the potatoes in a bowl and mash them using a potato ricer like the one shown here, or you can use a simple wire masher.

Ingredients

1.5 pounds (700 g) potatoes

2 tablespoons finely chopped parsley

7 ounces (200 g) canned tuna, flaked with a fork

½ cup (125 g) mayonnaise

pinch of salt

1 clove garlic, finely chopped

3 Add the tuna, garlic, and parsley to the bowl with the potatoes. Mix well. Season with salt to taste.

4 Put the mixture on a large serving dish. You can use your hands to mold the mixture into the shape of a fish.

25

TIPS & TRICKS
Ask an adult to help you move the pan of boiling water when draining the potatoes. Keep the mayonnaise in the fridge until you use it. Cold mayonnaise is easier to decorate with.

5 Decorate the fish with the mayonnaise. You can put the mayonnaise in a plastic bag. Cut a hole in one corner, and then squeeze the mayonnaise out. You can draw in the gills, fins, and scales.

Chocolate Cake

Italians love to finish a meal with a delicious chocolate dessert. If you love chocolate, too, this is the perfect recipe for you! This is a great cake to make when guests come for dinner. You could even make it for a friend's birthday. The dark chocolate gives this cake a rich flavor.

1 Place a large saucepan of water over a medium heat. Put the chocolate and butter in a smaller pan and place it in the larger one. Stir the mixture until it is melted.

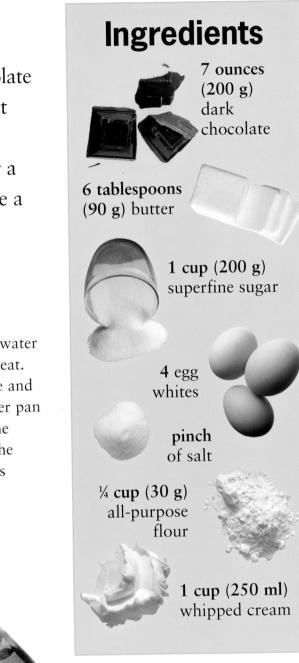

Ingredients

7 ounces (200 g) dark chocolate

6 tablespoons (90 g) butter

1 cup (200 g) superfine sugar

4 egg whites

pinch of salt

¼ cup (30 g) all-purpose flour

1 cup (250 ml) whipped cream

TIPS & TRICKS

Place the cake on the middle rack in the oven. Don't open the door during the first 20 minutes of cooking time, or your cake may go flat. Ask an adult to take the cake out of the oven. Ask an adult to help you separate the egg yolks from the whites, too.

2 Remove the saucepan from the heat. Add the sugar and stir until it has dissolved. Gradually add the flour, stirring until well mixed. Set aside to cool.

3 Beat the egg whites until stiff using a mixer. Add a pinch of salt before you begin so that the eggs stiffen quickly.

4 When the chocolate mixture is **lukewarm**, carefully mix in the egg whites. Use a spatula to gently blend in the egg whites.

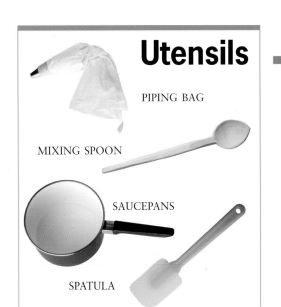

Utensils

PIPING BAG

MIXING SPOON

SAUCEPANS

SPATULA

5 **Grease** and flour a 10-inch (25 cm) cake pan and pour the mixture into it. Bake in a preheated oven at 300 °F (150 °C) for about 25 minutes. The cake should have a light crust but still be soft inside. To test if the cake is cooked, poke a skewer into the middle. If it comes out clean, the cake is ready. Remove from the oven and place on a wire rack to cool.

6 When the cake is cool, decorate it with the whipped cream. You can use a piping bag for this.

Tiramisù

(tee-rah-mee-SOO)

This dessert is so good that four different Italian regions—Lombardy, Emilia-Romagna, Veneto, and Tuscany—all claim to have invented it! It is fun to make and very tasty. When you serve it, your friends and family will think you are a gourmet chef. The name of this dessert means "pick me up."

1 Use the spatula to beat the egg yolks and sugar until they are creamy and light in color.

Ingredients

5 eggs, separated

⅔ cup (150 g) sugar

1 pound (500 g) mascarpone cheese

about 30 ladyfingers

1 cup (250 ml) strong black coffee

7 ounces (200 g) dark chocolate, grated

2 tablespoons (15 g) unsweetened cocoa powder

TIPS & TRICKS

If your local supermarket or Italian food store does not have mascarpone cheese, you can use the same quantity of cream cheese instead. This dessert needs at least 2 hours to chill in the fridge, so remember to start early. If you do not like the taste of coffee, use the same quantity of raspberry syrup instead.

2 Stir in the mascarpone a little at a time and mix well. In a separate bowl, beat the egg whites until they form a stiff mixture.

3 Carefully stir the beaten egg whites into the egg yolk and cheese mixture.

4 Dip the ladyfingers into the coffee quickly, so that they absorb a little but do not become too soggy.

5 Cover the bottom of a serving dish with a layer of the cream. Then add a layer of ladyfingers.

6 Use the spatula to spread the cream in an even layer.

7 Cover with another layer of cream and sprinkle with a little chocolate. Repeat until all the ladyfingers and cream have been used up.

8 Put the cocoa in a sieve and **sift** evenly over the top. Place in the fridge for at least 2 hours before serving.

Ice Cream with Chocolate Sauce

Having ice cream with hot chocolate sauce is one of the most delicious ways to finish a meal. Some believe ice cream originated in China, around 3000 BC. The ancient Chinese mixed snow with fruit and honey. As Europeans came into contact with the East, the secrets of making ice cream traveled to Europe. The technique of making smoother ice cream was perfected in Sicily in the 1500s. In Italy, ice cream is called *gelato*.

TIPS & TRICKS

If you do not have an ice cream maker, place the creamy mixture in a freezer-proof bowl and put it in the freezer. After 2 hours, stir quickly and put it back in the freezer. Repeat twice.

1 In a mixing bowl, beat the egg yolks and the sugar with a **whisk** until they are pale and creamy.

Utensils

WHISK

MIXING SPOON

SMALL SAUCEPAN

SAUCEPAN

ICE CREAM MAKER

Ingredients

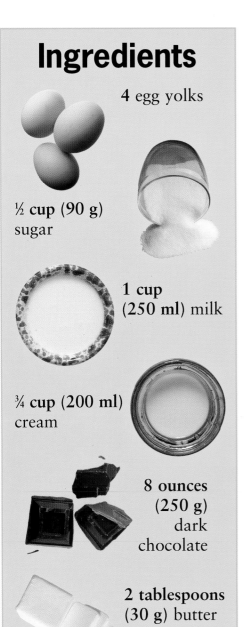

4 egg yolks

½ cup (90 g) sugar

1 cup (250 ml) milk

¾ cup (200 ml) cream

8 ounces (250 g) dark chocolate

2 tablespoons (30 g) butter

2 Add the milk and then half the cream gradually, beating all the time until they have been completely absorbed by the mixture.

3 Pour the mixture into the ice cream maker and follow the instructions to make the ice cream. If you do not have an ice cream maker, see the Tips & Tricks box for instructions on how to make ice cream by hand.

4 When the ice cream is ready, place the chocolate, butter, and remaining cream in a small saucepan. Put the small saucepan inside a larger one half full of water and place over medium heat until the ingredients have all melted together. Put the ice cream in a serving bowl and pour the chocolate sauce over the top.

Glossary

anchovies (AN-choh-veez) Small fish, often eaten salted and dried.

appetizer (A-pih-ty-zur) A dish served before the main course.

Arabs (AR-ubz) Natives of Arabia, an area located between the Red Sea and the Persian Gulf.

baguette (ba-GET) Baked French bread formed in the shape of a long stick.

coarsely chopped (KAWRS-lee CHOPT) Cut in larger pieces, not in fine, smooth pieces.

confetti (kun-FEH-tee) Small pieces of paper, thrown in the air at festive events.

dissolve (dih-ZOLV) To let a solid ingredient melt into a liquid.

drizzle (DRIH-zul) To let fall in fine drops or a fine stream.

grease (GREES) To coat a pan with oil or melted butter.

knead (NEED) To mix and smooth out dough before it is baked.

ladyfingers (LAY-dee-fing-gerz) Known in Italy as *savoiardi*. They are sweet, dried sponge cakes.

lukewarm (LOOK-WAWRM) Moderately warm.

Middle Ages (MIH-dul AY-jez) The period in European history between the late fifth century and the 1400s.

pasta (PAHS-tuh) Thin, unleavened dough, processed in many forms, such as spaghetti.

pinch (PINCH) The amount that can be held in the tips of two fingers.

Roman Catholic (ROH-mun KATH-lik) Part of the Catholic Church, which is led by the Pope.

saffron (SA-fron) The orange stigma of a crocus flower used for coloring and flavoring food.

sauté (saw-TAY) To fry food lightly in oil over medium heat.

serrated (SER-ayt-ed) Having a grooved edge.

sift (SIFT) To separate the coarse parts of a dry ingredient with a sifter.

sprinkle (SPRING-kul) To scatter in separate drops.

whisk (HWISK) A utensil used to whip food.

32

Index

Web Sites

Due to the changing nature of Internet links, PowerKids Press has developed an online list of Web sites related to the subject of this book. This site is updated regularly. Please use this link to access the list: www.powerkidslinks.com/lgc/italian/